Original title:
Currents of the Mind

Copyright © 2025 Creative Arts Management OÜ
All rights reserved.

Author: Julian Montgomery
ISBN HARDBACK: 978-1-80587-468-3
ISBN PAPERBACK: 978-1-80587-938-1

A Tidal Pool of Ideas

In a pool where thoughts splash wide,
Ideas bounce like fish that glide.
Some are bright, while others swim,
Flopping out, they make us grin.

Jellyfish of laughter float,
Tickling minds, they love to gloat.
Seashells whisper, secrets told,
Bubbles burst, ideas unfold.

Harmonics of the Heart

Beats of joy like drums in time,
Silly notes, a jester's rhyme.
Each note plucks a string of cheer,
Tickling fancies that bring near.

Chords collide in delighted play,
Laughter dances, come what may.
Melodies wrap with a chuckle's embrace,
Heartbeat's grooves, a jolly race.

Swirling Patterns of the Past

Old memories twirl like skirts in dance,
Twisting tales in a comical trance.
Clumsy falls and giggles galore,
Replays of moments we can't ignore.

Spinning tops of yesteryear,
Wobbling close, then disappear.
Laughter echoes as shadows play,
Reminding us of our silly way.

Sunlit Streams of Joy

Streams sparkle with giggles afloat,
Tickling toes in a paper boat.
Waves of mirth, they splash and glide,
Bubbling laughter, there's no need to hide.

Sunbeams dance on water's face,
Chasing ripples at a brisk pace.
Joy flows freely from heart to heart,
In this stream, we'll never part.

Mirrors of the Soul

In the mirror, I see a clown,
Juggling thoughts while wearing a frown.
Tickling my brain with a quirky show,
Reflections dance, but where do they go?

Bouncing ideas like a rubber ball,
Some flop and stink, others stand tall.
Laughing at shadows, chasing the light,
My mind's a circus on a whimsy flight.

The Flow of Time

Time's a river, but where's the paddle?
Floating on giggles, oh what a rattle!
Each minute a fish, wriggling away,
Caught in a net of what I say.

Hours swim by in a silly race,
Chasing my tail in a dizzying space.
Tick-tock, the clock has lost its mind,
Chiming along with the jokes unlined.

Intersecting Pathways

You take a left, I'll go straight ahead,
Lost in thought, or was that a thread?
Paths cross like noodles in a pot,
Al dente dreams, oh what have I got?

Steps wiggle like worms in the sun,
Laughing as we trip, oh this is fun!
Sideways thoughts and upside-down rays,
Navigating life in chaotic ways.

Ports of Perception

Docking thoughts at the port of glee,
Unloading giggles, won't you join me?
Boats made of laughter sail so high,
Anchored in whimsy, let's wave goodbye.

Loading emotions like cargo of dreams,
Navigating seas of chocolate streams.
Ports are abuzz with chatter and cheer,
Oh, what a trip to have you here!

Shifting Sands of Introspection

In the desert of my thoughts, I wander slow,
Searching for wisdom in a cactus show.
My brain's a squirrel, with no acorns in sight,
Juggling ideas like it's a circus flight.

Mirages dance like a lively charade,
While my focus spins, a funky cascade.
Dunes of doubt take a laughable stance,
As I stumble in my own cerebral dance.

Riptides of Realization

Caught in a wave of unfiltered glee,
Thoughts splash around, like fish in spree.
I dive for pearls that are lost in the sea,
Only to find it was my shoe, oh me!

Surfing on notions, they topple and spin,
Riptides of logic tug me, pulling within.
Yet here I float, with an anchor of jest,
In a pool of confusion, I simply rest.

A Pulse of Possibility

Heartbeat of dreams, it's a wild parade,
Ideas waltz by, in a silly charade.
Bouncing like rubber, my hopes take a leap,
Only to land in a pile of sheep.

Each pulse a giggle, a wink from the sky,
Imagination flies like a bird set to try.
With every heartbeat, a new path is spun,
Who knew that thinking could be so much fun?

Delicate Streams of Forgiveness

In a brook of blunders, I paddle my boat,
Waving at past woes, like a kid on a float.
Rocks of regret tumble into the stream,
But I giggle and splash, living the dream.

Each drop of 'sorry' dances with flair,
While laughter encircles the cool, crisp air.
Drifting on kindness, I float with a grin,
Forgetting my troubles, let the fun begin!

Rushing Waters of Intuition

In the stream of thoughts, I float,
A rubber duck lost, but full of hope.
A fish jumps high, wearing a hat,
It quacks like a frog, how about that?

My mind's a river, swirling and bright,
Eels doing the tango, what a sight!
Paddling past dreams in a canoe made of cheese,
Mice cheer with life vests, truly a breeze.

Waves of laughter crash and splash,
Goldfish philosophers, bold and brash.
A school of sardines sings a tune,
While jellybeans dance under the moon.

When thoughts collide, it's quite a show,
Bridges of giggles, they come and go.
Rushing waters, thoughts take flight,
In this silly stream, I feel just right.

Serenades of Silence

Whispers glide on fluffy clouds,
As squirrels form bands in the shrouds.
A quiet note in a still-filled room,
Sounds of giggles bloom like a spring bloom.

Beneath the calm, a mouse plays the flute,
As shadows of rabbits dance in pursuit.
Silent laugh breaks out like the dawn,
In the hush, a tickled giggle is drawn.

An orchestra of crickets in the night,
Their tiny symphony, a playful delight.
In this tranquil, yet funny affair,
The echoes of laughter hang in the air.

A serenade sung with whimsy and glee,
As secrets are shared by a silvery sea.
Hushed tones will not keep the humor confined,
In this playful quietude, joy is aligned.

The Flowing Canvas

Colors splash like a paintball fight,
A canvas of thoughts, oh what a sight!
Brush strokes giggle and twirl all around,
In this whirlwind of whimsy, joy is found.

Splashes of orange, green, and blue,
Each splash a thought, each thought a 'woo-hoo!'
A balloon floats by, with a grin on its face,
Dancing with colors in this joyful space.

A palette of giggles spills over the edge,
As brushes are tickled - they dance on the ledge.
The canvas chatters with every hue,
A masterpiece formed by the silly crew.

Shapes come alive, with laughter they bloom,
As the colors all sing in their joyful room.
In this flowing garden, creation's a spree,
Each stroke a fun twist of creativity!

Hidden Springs of Wisdom

In the hills of thought, springs bubble and flow,
Whispers of wisdom, don't say 'whoa!'
A wise old owl wears mismatched socks,
Riddles in riddles, he humorously mocks.

Beneath the surface, a treasure chest hides,
Filled with oddities, laughter abides.
A squirrel reads novels while munching on nuts,
And quotes silly wisdom, while doing the struts.

The springs shimmer bright with giggles galore,
As frogs philosophize on life down by the shore.
A magic hat floats by with a grin,
Telling silly secrets of where to begin.

In this playful realm where wisdom runs free,
Lessons are bubbly, like soda with tea.
Hidden springs keep the laughter refined,
In the depths of these pools, joy's intertwined.

The Labyrinth of Inner Waves

In a maze of thoughts I roam,
Chasing rabbits, none to clone.
A rubber chicken quacks a tune,
While I ponder what's for noon.

There's a parrot on my shoulder,
Whispering secrets, getting bolder.
It claims to know the truth about
Why my sock drawer's in a drought.

I trip on shoelaces of desire,
As thoughts drift like a kite on fire.
Silly ideas whirl about,
Like dancing clowns that scream and shout.

So I laugh amid the playful scene,
At the chaos that lives in between.
For in this labyrinth of sheer delight,
I find the fun in every fight.

Illumination in the Fog

A lightbulb flickers, dim and near,
While I grow a monster limb with cheer.
A specter of snacks calls my name,
In this fog, I forget the game.

Ghosts of thoughts drift like the mist,
Funky ideas I can't resist.
I stumble over my tangled dreams,
As laughter bursts at the seams.

Through the haze, I find a clown,
With a frown turned upside down.
He hands me popcorn, quite bizarre,
And rides off in a popcorn car.

So as the fog begins to clear,
I'll cherish the quirks that I hold dear.
Each moment's wisdom's wrapped in jest,
Illuminating my mental quest.

Flickers Beneath the Surface

Bubbles rise from thoughts below,
Like fish with wigs that steal the show.
A sunken treasure stands in line,
With socks that never match in twine.

My brain's a circus under waves,
Where silly monkeys plot and rave.
They juggle, dance, and break the rules,
In a ball pit filled with unruly fools.

A rover drifts through jelly beans,
He yells, 'Who knew dreams had means?'
I giggle at the comical plight,
As the ocean sparkles with delight.

So let's dive deep into the strange,
And flip our thoughts, let them exchange.
For beneath the splash is a world to find,
With flickers of joy in every mind.

The Stream of Unraveled Stories

A river flows with tales of yore,
Where socks and shoes dance on the floor.
Each splash a laugh, each wave a cheer,
As ducks on boats quack: 'What's for dinner here?'

I paddled past a giggling tree,
That spilled out cookies, wild and free.
Every branch holds a jester's laugh,
In the current of a silly path.

Tales of wiggly worms and cheese,
Bring giggles carried by the breeze.
In this stream, all worries fade,
As every turn brings a new charade.

So let the stories swirl and sway,
In a whirlpool of whimsy, let's play.
For in this flow, I truly find,
The joy that swirls within my mind.

Flux of Unspoken Dreams

In the realm where thoughts collide,
Socks on hands, we slip and slide.
Chasing wishes, lost in flight,
Dancing shadows in the night.

Every whispered joke, a spark,
Chortling giggles, lighting dark.
A bubble bath of silly schemes,
Floating high on vibrant dreams.

Pants on heads, we sway and dive,
Keeping secrets, oh so sly.
A world where nonsense takes its place,
With quirky smiles we embrace.

So let the laughter fill the air,
In this circus, without a care.
We'll ride the waves of silly streams,
And paddle through our waking dreams.

Hidden Streams of Emotion

Beneath the surface, bubbles brew,
With every twinge, a giggle too.
A hidden river, flowing fast,
Where feelings swim from first to last.

Who knew a sigh could sound so bright?
Tickles wrapped in morning light.
Tugging at the heartstrings tight,
Making joy burst out in flight.

Jokes that tumble like a stream,
Wobbling paths of blissful dream.
Each smile a curve, a point of bliss,
In this fun house, we can't miss.

So let the laughter underlie,
The twists and turns, we can't deny.
These streams of giggles, wide and free,
Are the quirky roots of you and me.

The Dance of Wandering Ideas

Ideas prance like lively birds,
Flapping wings without the words.
They twist and turn, a merry game,
Lost in thought, yet never tame.

A noodle dance, a wink, a nod,
Juggling clowns in thoughts so odd.
With every trip, a chance to play,
A carnival of minds on display.

Bouncing notions, round and round,
In this circus, truth is found.
Let's twirl along on tippy toes,
And see where this bright dance goes.

So partner up with whimsy's charm,
As thoughts entwine, we mean no harm.
In this goofy waltz, we'll find,
The laughter locked within the mind.

Shifting Sands of Perception

Sandy thoughts shift with the breeze,
Playing tricks, just like these bees.
They buzz around, and oh, what fun,
A sprinkle of nonsense in the sun.

Each grain a giggle, soft and sweet,
Shifting shapes beneath our feet.
A castle made of whimsy's hue,
Walls of laughter built for two.

With every wave that kisses shore,
A new idea, a joke galore.
Sifting through this mind's terrain,
Finding joy in every grain.

So let the tides of thought embrace,
In this grand, ridiculous place.
Where giggles shift, and smiles expand,
We're lost together in the sand.

The Meditative Storm

A thought-roof trembles, what a sight,
As ideas dance, oh, what a flight!
Pondering issues while flipping a fry,
I drop my spatula, and laugh at the sky.

Rain clouds chuckle, swirling bright,
Potatoes grin, in their pure delight.
With every thunder, a joke is spun,
Witty whispers drown the fun.

Mind twists and turns like a wet noodle,
Chasing logic like a caffeinated poodle.
Stormy thoughts? Oh, they're just a game,
After all, who needs to be sane?

So let it flow like a river of cream,
Frothy ideas in a nonsensical dream.
I sip my coffee, embrace the parade,
In this storm of silliness, no need for charades.

Whirlpools of Wisdom

I swirled my brain in a bubble bath,
With rubber ducks plotting their math.
Every splash is a clever plot,
They'll solve the world's greatest knot.

Sifting through thoughts like a funfetti cake,
Giggling at issues that make my head ache.
Wise owls hoot from the corner of my mind,
Teaching me knowledge while sipping on rind.

Round and round, all ideas twirl,
In a teacup ride, watch my brain unfurl.
A tangle of riddles, oh what a mess,
But biting my nails? Now that's a process!

Join the whirl, it's a laugh-a-thon,
With jelly beans guiding, we'll carry on.
Through whirlpools of nonsense, we will roam,
Finding wisdom in giggles as we make it our home.

Shifts in Perspective

I stared at my shoes; they looked quite odd,
Like they were thinking, 'Here's a flawed god!'
With every shuffle, a new face appears,
Laughing at wisdom found in my fears.

I tipped my hat to a cheeky raccoon,
Who said, 'Darling, don't take life too soon!'
Shift your gaze, squint at the stars,
You might find wisdom squirting from jars.

My socks have opinions on where I should go,
While my cereal whispers, 'Just take it slow.'
Shifts in my brain, they jive and dip,
I ride the waves on a lollipop trip.

So let's cartwheel through every odd thought,
Finding laughter in lessons that life has brought.
Twist and tangle, let's wiggle away,
In this silly dance, we'll be okay.

Echoes Beneath the Surface

In my head, a wave of jokes,
They swim like playful folks.
Fish with hats and silly ties,
Bubbling laughter fills the skies.

Thoughts dive deep, then float back up,
Like a fish that found a cup.
Every memory is a prank,
Making me feel quite the crank.

Swirling chaos, round and round,
Whirlpool of giggles, quite profound.
It's like a carnival in here,
Clowns and balloons, oh dear, oh dear!

Echoes of my mind do tease,
Like a ticklish breeze through trees.
In this ocean, absurdly bright,
I surf on waves of pure delight.

The Flow of Unseen Waters

Thoughts are like a river, wild,
Wiggly and often riled.
Silly ducks in grand disputes,
Arguing over rubber boots.

Flowing fast with laughter's quack,
Splashing jokes with quite the knack.
Paddle further, can't slow down,
I might just float into a town!

Underneath, where fishes play,
Each one with a joke to say.
Stream of giggles runs so free,
Join me in this funny spree!

So grab your gear and come afloat,
In my mind, there's fun to gloat.
Unseen waters, bright and clear,
Hold the laughter that we cheer.

Deep Currents of Memory

Beneath the surface, memories dance,
In silly hats, they take a chance.
A fish that tells a pun or two,
Sparks of joy in every hue.

Waves of past, they crash and flow,
Tickling thoughts that start to glow.
A current pulls on wistful dreams,
Where everything is what it seems.

Floating jesters in a stream,
In a frothy, laughing dream.
Splashing colors, bright and bold,
These memories, like tales retold.

Diving into depths so wide,
With every giggle as my guide.
In this ocean of good cheer,
Every wave brings laughter near.

Fragments adrift in Silence

In the silence, fragments roam,
Silly chatter finds a home.
Jigsaw pieces scattered 'round,
Funny shapes that make no sound.

A puzzle made from goofy sayings,
Bouncing thoughts, like kids, all playing.
Lost socks go on grand retreat,
Dancing with the unexpected beat.

Drifting memes on breezy tides,
Frolicking where laughter hides.
Each fragment tells a tale, it seems,
Whispering jokes from past daydreams.

And though in silence, here I stand,
The echoes tickle, oh so grand.
Fragments, mishaps, all align,
In my head, a comedy line.

Conduits of Composure

In a world where thoughts do float,
A rubber duck upon a moat,
With every splash, a giggle grows,
As sanity quickly ebbs and flows.

Thoughts skitter like a wayward cat,
Chasing shadows, what's up with that?
Each idea dons a silly hat,
Dancing round like a crazy brat.

Noodles twist in boiling air,
While worries vanish, do we care?
Life's punchlines leaping a few feet high,
As laughter lingers, who knows why?

So let your musings take a ride,
On roller coasters that slide and glide,
Find the fun in every flake,
And let your silliness awake!

Tempest of Thoughts

Lightning strikes a genius spark,
Caught inside a mental park,
Where squirrels lecture on the news,
While dreaming of their fancy shoes.

A tempest whirls inside the dome,
As spoken words begin to roam,
'Round and 'round like rollerblades,
Bouncing off the brain cascades.

Ideas clash like swords of cheese,
As laughter floats upon the breeze,
With every thought a dance routine,
The funniest sights you've ever seen.

So ride the waves of mental jest,
With thoughts that play, they're truly best,
Through storms of giggles, let us sail,
With winks and chuckles that never fail!

The Silent Stream

A stream flows gently, hush-hush,
With notes of whimsy, quick and plush,
It babbles soft like whispered dreams,
As fish wear hats and serve ice creams.

Voices echo, yet remain mute,
As turtles wear a business suit,
And frogs debate on topics deep,
While silly thoughts begin to leap.

The water tickles, how it plays,
And bubbles burst in funny ways,
Each drop a giggle, quick and spry,
Dancing 'neath a goofy sky.

So let the stream of laughter flow,
Where every thought can twist and glow,
In silence, jokes begin to gleam,
In this bright, quirky daydream!

Threads of Connection

In a web of vibrant strands,
Where merry madness lightly stands,
Threads weave in colors oh so bright,
As giggles flutter, taking flight.

Connections spark like fireflies,
Igniting wonder in the eyes,
Each tug a tickle, every pull,
Bringing thoughts that are quite dull.

Among the strings of silly fate,
Ideas dance and contemplate,
What if socks could sing a tune?
Or dessert was made from a balloon?

So stitch together every dream,
With laughter as the let's-all-scream,
In this fabric, fun unfolds,
Where all our quirks are worth their gold!

Unfurling the Invisible Flow

Thoughts like balloons in a breeze,
Float and bob with the greatest of ease.
One's going left, the other goes right,
Chasing squirrels in an endless flight.

Logic takes a vacation day,
While reason is down for a play.
A dance-off with chaos, what a sight!
Two left feet in the dead of night.

The chatterbox in my head won't hush,
It sings in the shower; oh, what a rush!
Dust bunnies join in the chorus, too,
Making soap bubbles burst with a "poof!"

I ponder the secrets of life with a grin,
But my sock drawer's the place I begin.
What colors clash? Who thought that was wise?
Aliens must've filled it with lies.

The Invisible Threads We Weave

In the attic of thoughts, dust flies everywhere,
Old socks and ideas hang up in mid-air.
A tapestry woven of giggles and sighs,
Where the yarn of my brain starts to tie up in lies.

Bits of wisdom are tangled in string,
Should I be a magician or just let them cling?
I'm searching for answers with no visible plan,
As a three-legged chicken prances on land.

Neurons collide in a wild game of chess,
The king held hostage, dressed in a mess.
Jesters and knights take charge of my dreams,
Their antics are funnier than they seem.

So here's to the chaos, the thoughts yet unseen,
Where humor may surface in moments obscene.
I find that the quirks of my psyche, dear friend,
Are the threads in this fabric that never will end.

Ripples in Thought

Splash! There goes an idea so bright,
It just dove in, what a wonderful sight!
Echoes of giggles skip across the lake,
While I ponder the choices I didn't make.

A noodle of logic, a crayon of sense,
Swirling in circles, it's all quite intense.
With each little twist, I chuckle and blink,
My thoughts have just taken a ride on the brink.

Like puddles of rain on a sun-drenched street,
Reflections parade in a comedic beat.
Waves of confusion? Oh, isn't it grand?
My brain's like a beach, with ideas in sand.

Laughter drifts gently on the warm breeze,
As my thoughts lounge about like a couple of peas.
So here's to the ripples, the giggles they sow,
In this pond of my mind, where I let myself flow.

Waves of Whimsy

From the shores of my dreams come wisps of delight,
Surfing on laughter, I take off in flight.
A seagull named Chuck squawks witty remarks,
As jellyfish jiggle with tiny blue sparks.

Thoughts tumble like surf as they crash on the shore,
Inventing new games I can't help but explore.
With a twist of my mind, I leap and I spin,
In a whirlpool of nonsense, that's where I begin.

A dolphin named Larry makes jokes on the waves,
Collecting the giggles that everyone saves.
Meanwhile, a crab zips by wearing a hat,
In this world of absurdity, how clever is that?

As I weave through the tides of this raucous parade,
With each burst of laughter, my worries all fade.
So let's surf the silliness, ride the wild tide,
In the oceans of whimsy, there's nowhere to hide!

The Confluence of Being

Thoughts collide like cars in a race,
Chasing their tails at a dizzying pace.
Ideas flicker like a faulty light,
Making sense of nonsense, oh what a sight!

Jokes swim around like fish in the sea,
Splashing and laughing, so carefree.
Doodles dance as they float through the air,
Tickling my brain, a whimsical affair.

Pondering life with a goofy grin,
Stumbling upon where the laughter begins.
A mind like a circus, chaos and cheer,
Juggling the madness, it's all quite clear!

So here's to the chaos, let's revel and shout,
In this wild party that's never in doubt.
With giggles and quirks, my thoughts take flight,
In this confluence of being, everything feels right.

Shadows Beneath the Surface

Whispers creep like shadows in the night,
Hiding secrets out of pure delight.
Tickling my fancy with stories so sly,
I giggle as thoughts just flit on by.

Beneath a calm facade where worries lurk,
Plotting mischief with a quirky smirk.
Ripples of laughter rise from the deep,
Where sanity's at stake, and thoughts leap!

Digging for gold in a muddy mind,
Finding treasures that are hilariously blind.
Funny little fables, absurdity thrives,
In these shadows, where humor survives.

So dance with the shadows, let's have a ball,
Beneath the surface, we'll smile and sprawl.
In every little nook, a chuckle awaits,
In the depths of our thoughts, fate happily prates.

Melodies of the Mind

A tune runs wild through the tangled mind,
Silly refrains are so easy to find.
Notes bounce along like squirrels in a tree,
Crafting a symphony that's jazzy and free.

Melodies clash like cats in a brawl,
Creating a ruckus, a free-for-all.
Laughter crescendos, then fades to a sigh,
As the rhythm of chaos just dances by.

Catchy little jingles that tickle the brain,
Making no sense yet so hard to contain.
Lyrical nonsense brings joy to the day,
In the melodies of madness, I'm swept away.

So hum along softly, let's skip down this path,
Dance with the rhythms, don't miss the laugh.
In the concert of nonsense, life takes its turn,
With the melodies of the mind, endlessly churn.

Fountains of Hope

Springs of laughter bubble and flow,
Gushing forth joys we barely know.
Witty words leap like frogs in the sun,
Splashing around 'till the day is done.

Tickling our fancy with whimsical glee,
Hope springs eternal, just wait and see.
From fountains of fun, we drink our fill,
Savoring sweetness that makes us smile still.

Jokes like rainbows arch over our heads,
Coloring thoughts where silliness spreads.
From puddles of laughter, we leap and we bound,
In this playground of thought, joy can be found.

So raise up your glass to this hope we create,
In fountains of mirth, let's celebrate fate.
For within every chuckle, a promise we weave,
In the tapestry of laughter, together we believe.

Depths of a Fluid Soul

Bubbles rise, thoughts float by,
A rubber duck starts to sigh.
Ideas swim in a silly dance,
Each wave whispers, "Take a chance!"

Silly fish wear hats and frown,
Chasing dreams that swirl around.
A jellybean takes the lead,
With every nibble, there's a need!

The ocean's watchful, eyes so wide,
It giggles softly, can't abide.
For every giggle, there's a splash,
Where deep thoughts and giggles clash!

So dive right in, don't be shy,
Make a puddle, wave goodbye.
In fluid realms, life's a jest,
A buoyant soul knows it's the best!

Tidal Imprints on the Shore of Being

Footprints dance upon the sand,
A crab joins in, it's quite unplanned.
Waves roll in with quirky glee,
Tickling toes, a jubilee!

Seagulls squawk in harmony,
Each note a laugh, a symphony.
As shells giggle, secrets spill,
The tide has rhythm, oh what a thrill!

Laughter echoes, sun shines bright,
The horizon's a playful sight.
In every inch, the jesters play,
Unraveling moments, day by day!

So build a castle, watch it sway,
Let imagination lead the way.
Within the tide's whimsical sway,
Life's imprints invite us to stay!

Blurred Lines of Perception

A tilted frame, a crooked view,
What's real? Maybe just a brew!
Wobbly thoughts, like jelly pies,
Giggles bursting, oh what a surprise!

A skewed horizon makes us grin,
Like socks that hug a wobbly chin.
Reality's a clownish jest,
Where logic's lost but fun is best!

Shadows dance and colors blend,
A twisty path with no clear end.
Each twist and turn reveals a theme,
Just when we look, we catch a dream!

So paint it bright, don't hold it tight,
Let loose the tangle, embrace the light.
In the haze, let laughter rule,
Through silly lines, we find the cool!

The Rise and Fall of Belief

Upward floats a thought once proud,
Then tumbles down, like laughter loud.
It hitches rides on whims and fancies,
In the circus of playful romances!

Like popcorn kernels in a pot,
Beliefs pop up, then change their spot.
A bubble burst, a giggle shared,
Life's silly moments, so unprepared!

Thoughts take flight on wings of jest,
Rising high, oh what a quest!
But swoosh, down they come with grace,
In the rollicking, playful race!

So cheer them on, the highs and lows,
With every laugh, a memory grows.
In the churning of a comical spree,
We find ourselves, so wild and free!

Glistening Reflections

In mirrors where thoughts can slide,
I see my brain take a joyful ride.
Dancing ideas like silly sprites,
Tickling neurons, oh what delights!

A thought pops up, like a jack-in-box,
Making me giggle, oh what a paradox!
Once I pondered my lost sock's fate,
Now I'm lost in a giggle state!

The fridge hums tunes of potential snacks,
While my mind plays tricks, oh what a fax!
Should I eat cake or solve a riddle?
Either way, I'll end up caught in a twiddle!

In bubbles of laughter, I float and sway,
Chasing ideas that come out to play.
Each quirk and thought a comedy show,
Leave the serious; let the giggles flow!

Comets of Contemplation

Rocketing thoughts, bright like a comet,
Shooting through space with a plummy flummox.
Why did I walk into that wall?
I ponder while laughing at my own fall!

My brain's a circus, elephants prance,
Clowns and acrobats join in the dance.
Juggling decisions, so hard to decide,
Should I nap or let my dreams ride?

Ideas whirl like candy in a breeze,
Tickling my senses, putting me at ease.
A fountain of giggles, a splash of delight,
Who knew my psyche could be such a sight?

But in the chaos, truths often appear,
That the best thoughts might bring silly cheer.
So I'll follow the comets, both wild and free,
In this galaxy of laughter, there's always me!

Edges of Epiphany

On the edge of a thought, I slip and slide,
Wobbling truths wearing a giggle disguise.
Eureka! Oh wait, that's just my shoe,
Tripping on wisdom, oh what can I do?

A genius burst comes with a giggly jest,
Maybe my brain just needs a rest.
While pondering broccoli's strange little tree,
I stumble on insights as silly as me!

Each epiphany bounces like a ball,
Chasing its tail in a comedic sprawl.
Jumping from thought to a donut instead,
Where snacks are the jewels that dance in my head!

So I chase these edges, giggling and free,
Where wisdom and nonsense both dance with glee.
In the world of my mind that's bright and absurd,
I laugh at the insights that seem just unheard!

Labyrinths of Longing

In the maze of musings, I seek a way,
Squirrels of longing dance and play.
Round every corner, a wish meets a chuckle,
Where hopes are wrapped in a cozy snuggle!

Through twisty paths, I trip and I tumble,
Dancing with dreams that make me grumble.
What do I want? A cat in a hat?
Or a cake with a joke that makes me go splat!

But the laughter echoes, I follow its trail,
Finding joy in each humorous fail.
Frolicking through wishes like butterflies bright,
In this funny labyrinth, everything's light!

Longing feels silly, like wearing a shoe,
That's too big for me, as I wobble through.
Yet as I wander, I find without strife,
That the giggles and dreams, they're part of my life!

Currents of Change

My thoughts are like a stock exchange,
Up and down, that's not so strange.
One moment I'm a serious sage,
The next I'm dancing on the stage.

A list of things I must complete,
Then lose my keys, it's bittersweet.
I plan a feast, I burn the bread,
Now it's just a snack instead.

In a maze of thoughts I dive,
Chasing dreams that come alive.
Wear a clown nose, make it real,
Life's a joke, that's how I feel.

Laughter echoes in my head,
Like a parade, but I'm misled.
On this ride, I'll take a chance,
Even when I trip and dance.

The River of Conscious Thought

Thoughts flow like a river wide,
With fish that giggle and reside.
One swims by with a silly grin,
While another pokes fun at my chin.

I ponder life while chewing gum,
Like a cowgirl who strums her drum.
Should I wear socks with my sandals?
Or just embrace my fashion scandals?

Ideas whirl like leaves in fall,
Some take flight while others sprawl.
A rubber duck floats near my head,
Quacking secrets I might have said.

Jump on in, let's make a splash,
Through waves of laughter, we will dash.
We might just find a treasure chest,
Filled with giggles; oh, what a jest!

Reeds in the Wind

Reeds sway gently, oh so neat,
Tickled by a breeze so sweet.
They whisper jokes in rustling tones,
About lost socks and silly phones.

A frog hops by with a witty croak,
He tells a tale of a funny bloke.
He jumped too high and hit a tree,
Now he's a comedian, can't you see?

The sun grins down with playful light,
As I twirl around, feeling bright.
Dance with me, let's sway some more,
Forget your worries, what's in store?

Giggles echo through the reeds,
Like in a garden of funny seeds.
So let's skip and whirl with glee,
For life's a joke; come laugh with me.

The Journey Within

I took a trip down memory lane,
Riding a train that's slightly insane.
A conductor with a rubber nose,
Said, "Welcome aboard, let's strike a pose!"

Through tunnels dark, I laughed and cried,
Met a squirrel with a crazy ride.
He recited poetry, quite absurd,
About his nuts and a flying bird.

The landscape changed, a circus scene,
Cotton candy clouds, so sweet and green.
Riding elephants, I cheered with glee,
Until I slipped and hugged a tree.

But oh, the fun this journey brings,
A rollercoaster of silly things.
So step aboard, it's all in stride,
The journey within is a joyful ride!

Cascades of Creativity

In the brain there lies a zoo,
With thoughts that dance and twirl like rue.
A monkey juggles balls of light,
While penguins plan a snowball fight.

The parrot squawks a brilliant scheme,
A watermelon makes a dream.
With colors bright, ideas bloom,
Like popcorn bursting in a room.

But wait! A cat, so sly and spry,
Steals the yarn of thoughts nearby.
Oh, how they roll and chase in glee,
A whirl of fun, just wait and see!

So let your thoughts break free and roam,
Like puppies lost, they'll find a home.
In laughter's tide, we surf and slide,
Embrace the chaos, let it ride!

The Flux of Ideas

Thoughts are like balloons in flight,
Some float high, some lose their bite.
A clown rolls past on a unicycle,
Shooting ideas like pop rockicle.

A pickle and a llama chat,
About the ways to wear a hat.
Quantum jumps from grape to cheese,
Explain the mysteries with such ease.

In a swirl of colors bright,
Ideas giggle 'til the night.
A rubber ducky quacks of fame,
While bubbles burst, it's all a game!

So don't be shy, let thoughts collide,
In a merry dance, we all can glide.
Like juice from fruits that burst and blend,
Ideas flow and never end!

Swells of Memory

A surfboard rides the waves of thought,
Where dreams and giggles intertwine, caught.
A fish in shorts asks, "What's the score?",
While jellybeans dance on the ocean floor.

Pudding cups take the finest dive,
As macaroni bands sing and jive.
The echo of a laughter spree,
Brings memories like sweet candy tea.

Turtles argue over who's more wise,
While candy corn reshapes the skies.
With each wave that rolls ashore,
Old jokes return for us to adore!

So ride the swells of smiles and glee,
Let old laughs flood in, wild and free.
In the tidal waves of what we reminisce,
Life's a funny slip, we can't dismiss!

Vortex of Visions

In a whirlpool, thoughts take flight,
Like a cat in socks, oh what a sight!
A squirrel debates with a rocking chair,
About the merits of fresh air.

Ideas churn like a creamy shake,
Laughter bubbling, what a mistake!
A jester juggles dreams so bright,
With cupcakes flying left and right.

Then comes a dragon, big and shy,
With toaster wings, he wants to fly.
His fire puffs marshmallow fluff,
Turning tough worries into just stuff.

So hold onto your hats, hold onto your dreams,
In this wild whirl, nothing's as it seems.
With giggles and joy, we'll spin and sway,
In the vortex of visions, we'll laugh all day!

Whispers of Thought

I ponder why cats avoid the bath,
As I chase dreams in a haphazard path.
They blink and ignore my wild ideas,
While I trip over shoes and laugh at my fears.

A squirrel in my garden steals my plans,
He hoards them away with his tiny hands.
I wonder if he dreams of grand feasts,
Or just collects snacks to share with his beasts.

Why do socks vanish in the wash's whirl?
Do they dance in the dark, take a twirl?
With my thoughts spinning 'round in a silly race,
I can't help but smile at the chaos I face.

In daydreams, I sprout wings and a crown,
While reality tells me to settle down.
Laughter erupts in the mess that I find,
In the circus of thoughts that boggle the mind.

Tides of Reflection

I thought I could cook an exotic dish,
But all I conjured was a burnt fish.
The smoke alarm sings a tune very clear,
While I dance on the floor, full of cheer.

I ponder why ice cream melts so fast,
Like my fleeting dreams that never last.
Imagine a scoop wearing a smile so wide,
As it drips down my arm on this wild ride.

Why do my plants only thrive on neglect?
In their wild, leafy world, they direct.
They plot against my green thumb with glee,
As I discuss life with the broccoli tree.

The clock ticks slow, like a snail on a spree,
In the race of my thoughts trying to break free.
But laughter leaps forth with every tick-tock,
As I witness the chaos from my old clock.

Waves of Serenity

I'd like to sail on a boat made of cheese,
Drifting through dreams, feeling the breeze.
With a crew of hot dogs and a wave of fries,
We'll search for the sea's most hilarious pies.

I try to meditate on a cloud for peace,
But the cloud keeps tickling with cotton release.
Thoughts play peek-a-boo, like a cheeky sprite,
While I chuckle aloud in the shimmering light.

Imagine a fish wearing a crown so grand,
Ruling the sea with a jellyfish band.
We dance through the bubbles and sing underwater,
While turtles roll by, making us laugh harder.

As waves crash high and laughter does swell,
In this ocean of whims, all is well.
Serenity floats in a joyful disguise,
While jokes ride the tide and laughter flies.

The stars above twinkle like playful bubbles,
Whispers of laughter amid life's small troubles.
I float on my thoughts, and the fun never ends,
In this sea of delight where imagination blends.

Ripples in the Stream of Consciousness

I skipped a stone, but it vanished so fast,
Into the depths of my mind's ocean vast.
Rabbits are dreaming of dancing in shoes,
While I'm lost in a daydream, unable to choose.

A peek into tea leaves revealed quite a sight,
The ghost of my grandma giving me fright.
She whispered of cookies from yesteryear's bake,
As I scribble nonsense for laughter's sweet sake.

What if my thoughts had a wild sense of style,
Wearing bright colors and dancing a mile?
With each silly whisper, a giggle ignites,
As I pondered the meaning of spaghetti fights.

In a river of whimsy where silliness flows,
I float on my raft made of gumdrops and prose.
The ripples of laughter ignite every quest,
In this stream of delight where nonsense feels best!

Dances in the Dark

In shadows where thoughts like to roam,
Silly whispers, they find a home.
Giggles echo, a playful fight,
Twilight waltzing, pure delight.

A hat on a cat, oh what a sight!
They dance with abandon, filled with light.
Jellybeans jive, with jellyfish blues,
In this moonlit chaos, they sing their views.

Twirling thoughts, a dizzying dream,
Like marshmallows floating in fluffy cream.
Laughter spills, a bubbling brook.
In the dark we giggle, come take a look!

The clock does a tango, tick-tock, do sway,
While night creeps in, chasing worries away.
Socks on our hands, we slip and slide,
Together we stumble, nowhere to hide.

The Language of Water

Bubbles giggle, they bounce and break,
Whispers of splashes, for laughter's sake.
Waves of waffle cone dreams do tease,
Rippling jokes like a light summer breeze.

A fountain of giggles, both loud and clear,
As puddles chuckle, 'We're glad you're here!'
The tap drips a rhythm, a soft little tune,
Dancing raindrops under a frowning moon.

Silly fish swim, wearing bright hats,
They speak in splashes, chit-chatting chats.
A swim in the pond, a slip oh so sly,
While ducks throw confetti, just passing by.

Giddy glimmers race in a stream,
Turning mundane dreams into ice cream.
In puddles mirth dances, with joy it plays,
The water sings loudly in splashy displays.

Stirring Springs of Passion

Bubbling fountains filled with delight,
Passion stirs softly, a cheeky sight.
Dancing cookies, they whirl and sway,
Baking up troubles, keeping them at bay.

A warm cookie hug, it cannot go wrong,
Jiggly laughter, a dance that is strong.
Brownies leap on the sunny side,
As cupcakes explode, they can't run and hide.

Frolicking flavors, they join the spree,
While sugar sprinkles lighten the tea.
Whipped cream giggles atop of the pie,
In this mad kitchen, let dreams fly high!

So stir the sweet smiles in pots of delight,
And serve up the joy in chocolate each night.
Life's simply scrumptious with laughter's embrace,
In stirring springs of passion, we find our place.

The Ripple Effect

A pebble tossed with a giggle so grand,
The ripples of laughter spread out on the sand.
Each chuckle a circle, expanding its way,
Making waves of joy that just can't stay away.

Silly smiles bounce like rubbery glee,
As silly squirrels whisper, 'Come join our spree!'
The pool of delight is a splashy affair,
Where joy starts to ripple, light as the air.

Running in circles, the giggle brigade,
They skip and they twirl, with no plan displayed.
From the tiniest chuckle to the loudest cheer,
All of us swimming, the fun's crystal clear.

The world is a carnival, spinning in jest,
With laughter as currency, we're truly blessed.
So let's toss our pebbles, come dance hand in hand,
Creating those circles, that ripple the sand.

The Undersea of Awareness

Bubbles rise from thoughts quite silly,
An octopus does dance and dilly.
With seaweed brains that twist and curl,
In this wet world, we all jump and swirl.

Fish swim past in bright attire,
Joking loudly, as if on fire.
A jellyfish drifts with goofy grace,
While crabs hold court in a funny place.

Seashell secrets, laughter hides,
Where coral reefs are joy-filled rides.
Oh, what fun beneath the waves,
In this ocean of giggles, one misbehaves.

So join the frolic, let's go explore,
In waters rich with tales galore.
Through bubbles of thought, we skip and prance,
In the undersea of awareness, we dance!

Threads of a Liquid Mind

With threads so thin, a web we weave,
Thoughts like spaghetti, you won't believe.
A knot here, a twist there, all in good fun,
As noodle brains race under the sun.

Silly string that dangles and flops,
We dive into pools of giggles that pop.
A mermaid sneezes, a big splash of laughs,
While fish in tuxedos recite silly drafts.

Watercolor dreams drift fast and float,
We swim in scribbles, a colorful boat.
With every stroke, a giggle erupts,
In liquid threads, life's joy interrupts.

Let's tangle our thoughts, in a whirlpool spin,
Where humor flows freely and we always win.
With each splash, we shed all we find,
In the threads of this quicksilver mind!

Ebbing Voices in the Dark

Whispers echo in the moonlight glow,
Chasing shadows, watch them go slow.
A ghost with a hiccup, a silly old dream,
In this dance of the night, we laugh till we scream.

Under the stars, the owls have a chat,
Discussing the latest trends in a top hat.
With every flicker, humor takes flight,
In the ebbing voices that fill up the night.

Laughter bubbles where silence should loom,
As crickets band together, they boom!
A jesting breeze makes the shadows sway,
In this darkened tune, we giggle away.

So join the chorus of chuckles and cheer,
With echoes of joy, we'll have no fear.
In valleys of laughter, let's make our mark,
Among ebbing voices that light up the dark!

Drifting Alongside Memories

On a river of playful thought we glide,
With memories like ducks on a casual ride.
Each quack a giggle, each splash a grin,
As past and present twirl and spin.

Float down the stream where time doesn't race,
With balloons of laughter, we float in space.
A rubber ducky leads the parade,
In a dance where every splash is made.

Nostalgia tickles, a featherlight tease,
While echoes of fun sway through the trees.
So grab a seat on this boat of renown,
And sail alongside foibles, wearing a crown.

With each gentle wave, we laugh and we cheer,
As memories drift, becoming quite clear.
In this playful stream, let's never be coy,
For drifting with laughter is purest of joy!

Navigating Stormy Seas of Thought

Waves of chatter crash and swell,
Thoughts like fish escape their cell.
Nautical maps all askew,
I can't tell what is false or true.

Lighthouse beams that flicker wide,
Guide me through this bumpy ride.
A seagull squawks, is that my brain?
Or just my lunch gone down the drain?

With each swell, I start to spin,
Captain of chaos, where to begin?
A shark named doubt begins to bite,
Yet here I am, I'll put up a fight.

But wait, what's that? A dolphin leaps!
Oh joy, my humor rarely sleeps.
I wave aboard, my crew's delight,
Let's sail through this storm—hold on tight!

Uncharted Waters of Intuition

In the sea of feelings, I reside,
Navigating whims on a bumpy ride.
A compass spins, is that my gut?
Or just my lunch trying to erupt?

Mysteries swirl like a school of fish,
Swimming around each ungranted wish.
I ask the octopus for direction,
It gives me eight confusing reflections.

A buoy bobs, it's hard to think,
What was I saying? Oh, pass the drink!
Mermaids giggle and tease my thought,
"Relax, sailor, it's wisdom you sought!"

With nets of jest, they cast away doubt,
I laugh so loud, I might just shout.
This ocean's wild, yet feels just right,
Come join me here, in the tangled light!

Beneath the Cascading Thoughts

Rivulets of wonder start to flow,
Thoughts trickle down, a comic show.
A waterfall of what could be,
Drowning in laughter, quite carefree.

Pebbles of worry bounce along,
Yet here I am, I sing my song.
A fish jumps up, it winks and grins,
"Life's a splash; let's dive in!"

Cascades of giggles fill the air,
Each drop a joke, I just stop and stare.
What's this? A turtle wearing a hat?
A curious sight—imagine that!

I ride the flow, I twist and turn,
In this stream, I feel I learn.
The water sings, it bubbles bright,
Join me, friend, in this sheer delight!

Moonlit Paths of Contemplation

Under the moon's bright, silvery glow,
Thoughts wander like shadows, to and fro.
What was I pondering just a while ago?
Oh right, why don't cats ever say no?

Each step I take leads to what's absurd,
A pondering heart, so unperturbed.
The stars giggle, they're in on the joke,
While crickets play tunes that tickle and poke.

I spot a raccoon, wise beyond measure,
He's raiding my trash, a true little treasure.
"Reflect on your dreams, don't worry so fast,
Life's a buffet, eat well, have a blast!"

Through paths that spiral, I roam and laugh,
Every turn leads to a new photograph.
So let's stroll along, just you and I,
In this moonlit maze where wonders lie!

Tides of Reflection

I stared at my reflection, quite perplexed,
It winked back at me, feeling quite vexed.
My hair did a dance, all wild and free,
I laughed at the mirror, tough luck for me.

Thoughts drift on waves, like boats on a spree,
One's sailing for dinner, another for tea.
With every bobble, a giggle escapes,
Who knew deep thoughts come in such funny shapes?

In the ebb and the flow, a joke takes its stand,
My brain's got a beach ball, stuck in the sand.
It bounces and tumbles with glee in the sun,
Making silly plans, oh what silly fun!

So here's to those moments, bizarre yet true,
Where laughs are the best, and thoughts feel brand new.
Dive deep in your dreams, let your humor ignite,
For life's greatest jokes come from out of the night.

Streams of Consciousness

A river of thoughts, so quick and extreme,
Flowing past my brain like a wild, wacky dream.
One moment I'm here, the next I'm not there,
Just swimming in tangents, but I don't have a care.

There's fish in my brain, swimming all day,
The truth is a catch, but they swim far away.
With nets made of laughter, I try to reflect,
On the silly little things that my mind can't detect.

I ponder the meaning of socks left alone,
The missing one jumps and just won't be shown.
As thoughts start to bubble, a giggle emerges,
What if my socks have their own little urges?

And as I float on this stream full of cheer,
Every twist and each turn brings a chuckle so near.
Join me in laughter, let your thoughts run wild,
In the rivers of nonsense, we're all just a child.

Undercurrents of Dreams

Underneath the surface, where odd thoughts lurk,
Giggling fish giggle, they know how to work.
They whisper of dreams, so silly and bright,
I chase them at dawn, in the morning light.

I dreamt I was flying on a chicken's back,
We soared over hills, in a fluffy attack.
But just as I thought I was king of the air,
That chicken had plans, and I lost my fair share.

With waves of absurdity washing ashore,
I dive deep for treasures, but find lots of lore.
The couch is a mountain, the dog is a beast,
In the land of my dreams, the funny never ceased.

So grab your imagination, let's sail on this sea,
Where humor reigns high, and we laugh wild and free.
With every wave crashing, a grin is released,
In the undercurrents of dreams, joy's never ceased.

Flows of Emotion

Emotions are rivers, with rapids and glows,
Sometimes they're laughter, sometimes they pose.
One second I'm happy, next I might pout,
Just like a stream, I'm always about.

A twist of affection, a turn of delight,
Like rolling and tumbling, from morning till night.
A splash of excitement, that tickles my toes,
In flows of emotion, the funny side grows.

Pour joy like a fountain, let it cascade,
While worries float by on a silly charade.
The world is a playground, getting mad is absurd,
When laughter in rivers is the best kind of word.

So dance in the streams, let your heart feel the beat,
With every dip and dive, make your journey complete.
In this wacky parade, we all share the ride,
For life's sweetest moments, let your humor decide.

Fractals of Feeling

My thoughts do somersaults, oh what a sight,
Like pizza dough flying, up high, take flight.
Confetti of giggles in a wild parade,
Pancakes of worries, all buttered and laid.

I juggle my notions, they slip and they slide,
Like cats on a skateboard, with nowhere to hide.
Fractals of laughter, forever they spin,
With sprinkles of joy, I'm all grinned within.

A dance with my thoughts, a tango of glee,
Like frogs in a disco, just bouncing, you see.
Balloons filled with wonders, they pop and they gleam,
In this circus of feelings, I twirl and I beam.

So bring on the whirlpool, the twist and the shout,
My thoughts take a dive, bouncing in and out.
In a kaleidoscope mixed, where the sillies unwind,
Life's a comedy sketch, oh what's on your mind!

Nebulas of Nostalgia

Once I misplaced my socks, what a grand scheme,
They wandered for miles, or so it would seem.
Mixing memories like cereal in milk,
Try to catch the past – it's as smooth as silk.

Sprinkled with laughter, oh how we roam,
To find old diaries, we call them home.
With pixie dust sprinkled on ancient tales,
Like fish in a bowl, spinning never fails.

Oh, the flavor of childhood, like bubblegum sweet,
Where giant lollipops grow under our feet.
Sailing through time on a boat made of cheer,
With nostalgia as wind, how lovely, my dear.

These nebulas twirl, like a merry-go-round,
In a galaxy bright where giggles abound.
So let's toast to moments, however they shine,
In the laughter of ages, I'll always call mine!

Tangles of Time

Tick-tock goes the clock, but do I care?
I'm tripping on seconds, it's quite the affair.
Like spaghetti on Sundays, all twisted and round,
These tangles of time are delightfully found.

With calendars dancing, they fumble and sway,
Each month's a new prank, what game will they play?
Like cats on a roof, they prance and they fight,
Oh, the shenanigans of day into night.

Days ride like roller coasters, up and down,
Each moment a jester, wearing a crown.
The minutes do backflips, the hours, they gleam,
In this circus of time, we're living the dream.

So take off your watch, just toss it away,
Let's tango with moments, come join in the fray.
In these tangles of time, we giggle and glide,
For in laughter, we find the adventures inside!

Patterns of Connection

In a world of pixels, where memes come alive,
Our thoughts mingle like muffins, just waiting to thrive.
Connections like spaghetti on a plate,
All twirled and twisted, it's truly first rate.

Friendship's a bonbon, wrapped up in laughter,
With sprinkles of love, it's what we're after.
Like bees in a garden, we buzz and we beam,
Creating sweet honey from each silly dream.

A tap of a button, and here's the delight,
We share our funny stories, from morning to night.
These patterns of bonding, a dance on the screen,
With cat videos popping, it's our daily routine.

So raise a device, let's make it a toast,
To connections that sparkle, they matter the most.
In a mix of our quirks, together we shine,
Life's a patchwork of joy, forever entwined!

The Spiral of Knowing

Round and round, my thoughts do twirl,
Like a cat chasing its tail in a whirl.
Each revelation, a tumble and roll,
My brain's a circus, in full control.

Ideas spring forth, a jolly old dance,
Juggling notions, they skip and prance.
Wisdom is funny, like a clown in a hat,
Tickling my neurons—imagine that!

Winding like noodles on a plate of joy,
A spaghetti feast, oh what a ploy!
Each thought a meatball, some saucy surprise,
Making me chuckle, and oh, how time flies!

So here we go, with a giggle and sigh,
In this spiral, I float, as the pixels fly.
Life's a stand-up, where all jokes align,
And I laugh at my wisdom, feeling just fine.

Bridges of Understanding

Building bridges with thoughts on a whim,
Constructing pathways, not bold but dim.
Each plank a pun, with humor it bends,
Connecting the dots where logic extends.

Underneath arches of playful intent,
Words flow like water, no need to repent.
I trip on my tongue, then laugh as I fall,
For understanding is funny, not grand at all.

Each step a joke, on this rickety line,
Balancing wisdom with lashes of twine.
Who knew the journey could tickle my sides?
While building my bridges, my laughter abides.

So come join the fun on this illustrious path,
Where all roads are paved with a mirthful laugh.
Embrace the absurd, for it's part of the plan,
In bridges of thought, let our giggles span!

Rains of Revelation

Droplets of wisdom fall from the sky,
Each splash a giggle that catches the eye.
Puddles reflect, in distorted glee,
Revelations that dance like a bumblebee.

Storm clouds gather, but I'm not afraid,
As lightning ignites my thoughts in cascade.
Umbrellas of laughter uphold my mind,
Showering insights, both silly and kind.

The sun peeks out, in a jovial jest,
Turning raindrops to prisms, a colorful fest.
Nature's a comedian, with punchlines that play,
In rains of insight, let's jump and sway!

So dance in the droplets, let joy be your guide,
For every splash is a tickle inside.
Embrace the wet wisdom that woos us to grin,
And splash in the hilarity, let the fun begin!

Driftwood Thoughts

Floating through the sea of my mind's uncharted bliss,
Driftwood thoughts bobbing, each one hard to miss.
Some weigh like anchors, while others just float,
Like rubber duckies on a whimsical boat.

Ideas wash ashore, from distant lands bright,
Glistening like treasures, a sheer delight.
They intertwine and tumble, as waves give a cheer,
Tickling the shore with a giggle, oh dear!

Each stick is a story with a punchline or more,
Curly and twisty, like old ocean lore.
Waves of humor crash, making splashes with glee,
Driftwood thoughts whisper, "Come laugh along with me!"

So let's sail on this sea, where silliness swells,
In driftwood adventures, where each one compels.
With laughter as our compass, we'll navigate the spree,
On a whimsical journey, just you and me!

Cascade of Uncertainty

I woke up today, where's my sock?
Did it run away, or hide like a clock?
Worry on a rollercoaster, round and round,
Just when I think it's lost, it's finally found.

Dancing with thoughts like clumsy ballet,
Twisted in circles, they just won't play.
Trying to catch a breeze with a net,
It's slippery fun, but what'll I get?

A brain full of jelly, wiggly and bright,
What's for lunch? Can I book a flight?
Balloons in my head, they float and they pop,
What I really want is a never-ending hop!

So here in this chaos, laughter will spark,
Each silly thought is a bouncing lark.
Cascading dreams, in echoes they blend,
Oh, what a whirlwind, on that we depend!

Vibrations of the Heart

Beating like drums, my thoughts spin around,
A joke in the silence, a giggle profound.
Why did the chicken, oh why did it dare?
To cross the road with no single care?

Whispers of love in a hiccuping tune,
Like dancing with ducks under the light of the moon.
What's this sensation? A tickle, a cheer?
It's just my emotions, I'm happy, sincere!

Laughing out loud at the quirks of my head,
Thoughts like confetti, they dance and they spread.
A tango with mishaps, a breeze full of glee,
This heart is a stage, come tango with me!

Vibrations of joy, what a crazy flight,
Daydreaming whimsical, everything feels right.
With chuckles and snorts, I embrace every part,
In this funny game, I'm the queen of my heart!

Echoes in Solitude

In the quiet of night, I hear whispers and creaks,
What's that sneaky shadow? My brain just peaks.
Tick tock, thinks the clock, where shall I roam?
Is it time for a snack, or should I go home?

Echoes of laughter that bounce off the walls,
Like bouncy balls thrown in empty halls.
Solitude's funny, it teases my mind,
With giggles and grumbles, so intertwined.

Pajamas and cereal, my late-night gear,
Talking to pillows, 'Oh dear, oh dear!'
Every thought's a jester with a cheeky grin,
The silence of night is where fun begins.

Alone but not lonely, I dance in my chair,
With echoes of nonsense floating in air.
In this stillness, I find a wild delight,
Laughing with shadows until morning light.

Mists of Meaning

Foggy thoughts drift like clouds on a spree,
Where are they going? Oh, let them be free!
Misty ideas that swirl and they weave,
What's hidden in haze? I just can't believe!

Searching for clarity in this cloudy sea,
A rainbow of nonsense is waiting for me.
What is the meaning of cat videos, friend?
Just laughter and joy that seem to transcend!

I ponder and ponder; it's quite a fun mess,
Finding bright treasures in puzzling stress.
With giggles in whispers, the mists may align,
Unraveling wonders, each thought a design.

In the fog of confusion, I frolic and play,
Riding the waves of my mind's silly sway.
Mists of a meaning, elusive and bright,
Bring laughter and whimsy, sweet as the night!

www.ingramcontent.com/pod-product-compliance
Lightning Source LLC
Chambersburg PA
CBHW062108280426
43661CB00086B/333